>> CODE POWER: A TEEN PROGRAMMER'S GUIDE™

GETTING TO KNOW

Alice

JEANNE NAGLE

rosen publishing's
rosen
central®

NEW YORK

Published in 2015 by The Rosen Publishing Group, Inc.
29 East 21st Street, New York, NY 10010

Copyright © 2015 by The Rosen Publishing Group, Inc.

First Edition

Library of Congress Cataloging-in-Publication Data

Nagle, Jeanne, author.
Getting to know Alice/Jeanne Nagle.—First edition.
     pages cm.—(Code power: a teen programmer's guide)
Audience: Grades 5 to 8.
Includes bibliographical references and index.
ISBN 978-1-4777-7693-3 (library bound)—ISBN 978-1-4777-7695-7 (pbk.)—
ISBN 978-1-4777-7696-4 (6-pack)
1. Alice (Computer program language)—Juvenile literature. 2. Object-oriented programming (Computer science)—Juvenile literature. 3. Three-dimensional display systems—Juvenile literature. 4. Virtual reality—Juvenile literature. I. Title.
QA76.7.N34 2015
005.1'17—dc23
     9391

                                                                    2013043305

Manufactured in the United States of America

{CONTENTS

Once upon a time, in 1865 to be exact, British author Lewis Carroll wrote a book that has since become a classic of children's literature: *Alice's Adventures in Wonderland.* The book told the story of the title character's journey to an amazing place filled with unusual sights and interesting creatures and beings. Throughout the tale, Alice experiences several events that defy logic. Responding to several somewhat mysterious commands, she winds up changing size, playing games, and attending a tea party. As it turns out, her adventure was a dream; it was all just a story made up in her head while she was sleeping.

Once upon another time—some 140 years after Carroll's book was first published—a group of computer scientists, researchers, and software engineers developed a computer programming environment called Alice, named in honor of the girl in the story. Designed to help beginners learn computer programming, Alice the software lets users create

>> An illustration from *Alice's Adventures in Wonderland*. Alice Educational Software is named after the heroine of this book.

virtual worlds with colorful, three-dimensional settings and characters. This Alice uses logic, not defies it. Dragging and dropping tiles filled with prewritten strings of commands makes the on-screen characters come to life and perform all sorts of tasks. In the end, being able to animate whatever worlds they come up with is a dream come true for beginning programmers using Alice.

The differences between the two Alices are pretty obvious. One is a human girl (or at least the character of a young girl), whereas the other is a piece of computer technology. The main similarity between them, however, is more revealing. Carroll's Alice and the programming language of the same name rely heavily on the art of storytelling. Instead of relying on a book format, however, the programming software lets users share stories by creating short animations.

"We like to refer to it as Pixar in your garage," says Randy Pausch, former director of the Alice Project at Carnegie Mellon University in Pittsburgh, Pennsylvania.

The software was developed to ease users into computer programming by making it creative and fun. Users not only learn basic programming, but they also sharpen their math and logic/problem-solving skills, all while enjoying themselves. Projects they can create include animated movies, videos, and even simple games. The possibilities are seemingly limited only by a user's imagination. Students in a computer science class at Duke University in Durham, North Carolina, created an animated nine-hole miniature golf course, complete with a smoking volcano. Other projects created by novice programmers include dance videos and interactive greeting cards.

Millions of users have downloaded, for free, the software since it first became available to the general public. The programming environment is used as a teaching tool in college, high school, and even middle school classrooms across the United States and in various parts of the world. This degree of popularity can only mean one thing: Computer programming for beginners is no longer a "once upon a time" proposition— it is very much in the here and now using Alice.

CHAPTER 1

ALICE TO THE RESCUE

Wh
hen it comes to having fun with computers, most people think of playing games, chatting with their friends, and posting to social media sites. Programming and writing code, which can be time-consuming and requires painstaking attention

>> Using computer programs is an everyday fact of life for business and communication. Coding is a rarer skill, but one that is increasingly being taught at an early age.

to detail, would most likely not jump to mind. Only computer scientists, whose job it is to write code that makes computers perform various tasks, could possibly add programming to the list of enjoyable activities, right?

Not so fast. Programming has come a long way since the first computers were built and put to work. Several coding languages and software platforms have been designed to introduce people to the art of computer programming by making the task fun. Among these is Alice Educational Software, known simply as Alice.

EMERGING FROM THE RABBIT HOLE

At the beginning of the twenty-first century, the number of students enrolled in college-level computer science degree programs had dropped significantly from previous years. Even students who were interested in the field were finding it difficult to master writing code. Some people compared programming to "falling down a rabbit hole"—an expression, borrowed from *Alice's Adventures in Wonderland*, that means entering a strange and difficult situation from which it is not easy to escape. Because they had trouble learning to program, many students gave up on computer science after the first few classes in the subject and chose another major.

Fewer students studying computer science meant fewer professionals able to create, fix, and maintain computer programs that people the world over had come to depend upon. The result of fewer computer scientists could mean a slowdown or even an

>> In Pittsburgh, Pennsylvania, Carnegie Mellon University, the birthplace of the programming software that became known as Alice.

outright stoppage of the ways in which people conduct business, socialize, communicate, and entertain themselves.

A group of computer scientists at Carnegie Mellon University recognized what was happening in the field and decided to take action. While working at the University of Virginia in Charlottesville, Virginia, Professor Randy Pausch had started developing a three-dimensional (3-D) animation computer program that would help him teach graduate-level gaming and animation students. This was the original version of Alice. Pausch brought the technology with him to Carnegie Mellon University

>> ALICE AND *THE LAST LECTURE*

Randy Pausch is known for more than being the originator of Alice. After learning that he had terminal pancreatic cancer in 2006, Pausch went back to the University of Virginia as a guest lecturer. His presentation became a viral video sensation and a best-selling book called *The Last Lecture.*

During the inspirational presentation, titled "Really Achieving Your Childhood Dreams," Pausch emphasized the importance of reaching for and achieving goals. He also covered how helping others achieve their dreams could be even more rewarding than achieving one's own.

In his lifetime—Pausch died in 2008—he certainly helped hundreds, if not thousands, of students achieve their dream of becoming computer scientists, thanks in large part to Alice. During his last lecture, Pausch spoke proudly of his work on Alice as being a professional legacy of sorts. "[T]o the extent that you can live on in something," he said, "I will live on in Alice."

in 1997. There, he and a team of faculty and students adapted the original Alice software, creating a method that would ease beginners into computer programming by making it less complicated. This second version, Alice 2.0, became the basis for the software platform used by beginning programmers today.

As of 2013, beginning programmers had the option of working in Alice 2.x and the slightly more advanced 3.x. The "x" in each case stands for various subversions of the software's releases.

WHAT A DRAG

Alice 2.0's creators knew that many beginning programmers abandoned or avoided computer science classes because they

>> Traditional programming meant carefully keying in a bunch of code. Users of Alice are more apt to use a computer's mouse than a keyboard when writing programs.

found it hard to write traditional code. Programming languages such as Fortran and Java consist of line upon line of numbers, letters, and punctuation marks that have to be written in a very precise order for them to work properly. One false keystroke and the code is ruined, making it impossible for the computer to do what the user wants it to do until the error is discovered and fixed.

Alice is one of several newer programming environments that use prewritten code contained in graphic tiles, which beginners can drag and drop from an online menu onto a workspace, which in Alice is called a code panel. Alice's code tiles contain statements that include instructions for animation, such as "move" and "turn." These are known as methods. There are also command tiles, including "do in order" and "do together," which dictate the order in which the methods should take place on-screen.

OBJECTS OF ALICE'S AFFECTION

In programming, an object is a collection of data, or information, stored in a computer's memory. The properties of the object tell the computer things like what the object should look like, what the various parts of the object are, and where the object is supposed to be located. Another way to look at properties is to think of them as parts of objects that can be changed in some way. Objects in Alice are the characters, backgrounds, and various other items on-screen.

Alice is considered an example of object-oriented programming (OOP)...sort of. Computer scientists have strict rules and guidelines concerning what a true OOP platform is, and there has been some debate about whether or not Alice meets all of those requirements exactly. However, when it comes to the basics, Alice can certainly be defined as an OOP platform because objects, which are created by users, perform all of the actions and jobs that users program them to do.

ALICE GETS ALONG WITH EVERYONE

The Alice Project team could have kept the design of Alice software to themselves and used it to teach students at Carnegie Mellon and other participating universities only. But that would have gone against the spirit in which the resource was created. The developers wanted to make sure that many students took an interest in computer science, not just the young adults in their own academic community. As its creators, the team could have shared the software but charged for it. Instead, they made Alice open-source, which means there are no fees, costs, or licenses involved.

No special equipment, or a particular kind of computer, is necessary to make Alice work either. The software is designed to run on PCs and Macs, desktops and laptops, and is compatible with Windows XP, Vista, Windows 7, Mac OSX, and Linux operating systems. Alice is downloaded from the Internet.

>> A row of laptops, ready for sale. No matter the make or model, virtually every computer enjoys compatibility with Alice downloadable software.

Accessing it is as simple as going to the Carnegie Mellon site (www.alice.org) and downloading the software.

A minimum of 1 GB of RAM is required to download and run Alice. Users would benefit from working on a computer with a 3-D video card because it enhances the speed of running animations, but a 32-bit VGA graphics card should work just fine. The software's creators recommend using a desktop or laptop computer to run the software, since most netbooks are not equipped for optimum display of Alice's 3-D graphics. Alice 3.1

is not meant to be run on smartphones, tablets, other portable devices, or through gaming consoles. Some users report that the local version fits on, and can be operated from, a 256-MB flash drive, so portability should not be an issue.

To help teachers use Alice in their classrooms, Carnegie Mellon offers an array of tools geared toward educators. These include textbooks, lecture notes, suggested labs, videos, and annual workshops.

>> A LITTLE HELP FROM SOME HIGH-POWERED FRIENDS

Through the years the creative team behind Alice has had financial and other assistance from a number of sources. The support of these organizations and corporations has not only helped the team at Carnegie Mellon develop and launch Alice software, but it also has contributed to the development of teaching materials and the growth of the project's Web presence.

Three U.S. government agencies—the National Science Foundation (NSF), the Defense Advanced Research Projects Agency (DARPA), and the National Aeronautics and Space Administration (NASA)— were early backers, as were Chevron, Python, Pixar, and Microsoft Research. Other technological entities and computer companies, which have a vested interest in the future of computer science, also have a hand in Alice's creation and success. These include Google, Intel, Science Applications International Corporation (SAIC), and more recently, Sun Microsystems. Other sponsors include Disney, Oracle, Hyperion, and various charitable foundations.

WORLDS APART

Because they are alternate universes populated by beings, landscapes, and situations that spring from each user's mind, the animations created by Alice users are referred to as worlds. There are a number of factors that set the worlds of Alice—and indeed, Alice in its entirety—apart from other programming environments.

LESS SYNTAX, MORE LOGIC

Traditional, or procedural, computer programming revolves around syntax—the complicated rules that determine the order in which code must be placed for a program to run smoothly, or even run at all. All the letters, numbers, and punctuation marks that go into writing procedural code must be keyed in by a programmer in the exact right order.

Code is already written and placed in Alice's graphic tiles. Because they don't need to fret over the correct syntax, Alice programmers are free to concentrate on the logic of the programs they are building. In computer programming, logic has to do with how commands, or instructions, are set up to perform certain tasks. In other words, Alice lets beginning programmers focus less on the nitty-gritty of syntax and more on the big-picture vision of how their programs are going to operate.

SEEING IS BELIEVING, AND LEARNING

One advantage of not dealing with syntax comes into play when users test their programs. Often when there is a syntax error in keyed code, programmers have to review pages filled with strings of letters, numbers, and punctuation marks to locate where the missing or misplaced element is. This is a time-consuming process.

Alice eliminates the need to go on a syntax hunt because of its visual, object-oriented nature. When a program experiences problems, users can see exactly what is happening on-screen, rather than just being told there is a syntax error. Finding the instructional graphic tile at fault and replacing it with the correctly coded tile is a lot easier, and quite a bit quicker, than trying to find the trouble spot in a string of code.

DIMENSIONS OF DIFFERENCE

Alice is not the only simplified computer programming language on the market, but it has a feature that sets it apart from similar programs such as Scratch and Greenfoot: 3-D graphics used for storytelling purposes. Creating movies in a 3-D environment makes characters and other objects look more real, thereby enhancing the program experience for users and viewers.

Last but not least, the fun factor involved in being creative and telling stories sets Alice apart from traditional programming methods as well.

CHAPTER 2

A WONDERLAND OF OPPORTUNITY

To users, the animations created in Alice are more than just simple little movies. They are expressions of creativity and stories shared, not to mention the result of their beginning adventures in computer programming. They are, as the software calls them, worlds. All the action in Alice takes place in an integrated development environment, or IDE, which in simple terms is the software application that provides the tools that make programming in Alice possible.

The ability to tell stories via animation is a huge reason why Alice is so popular. In 2009, when Alice 3 was released in its trial version, Alice 2.2 was being used by an estimated 15 percent of colleges and universities in the United States. That number doesn't include high schools and middle schools that had downloaded the software. Yet it is important not to overlook the original reason why the platform was created—to help teach computer programming.

The success of Alice as a teaching tool is not only because of its ease of use, but also because of the way in which it presents essential programming concepts. Users can connect what

>> A teacher at a technology camp in the United Kingdom introduces secondary school students to computer programming.

is happening on-screen with the specific instructions they give to objects, thereby learning the way that commands control the action within a program. Many of the same terms used in traditional, or general-purpose, programming have made the jump to the Alice programming language. In this way, users become familiar with the vocabulary that advanced programming requires—or, to put it another way, they get to know the "language of the language."

Following is a brief overview of how Alice 3.0 works. Included are many of the programming concepts and terms that users are introduced to when using the software.

OPEN SESAME!

When users open Alice, a welcome box appears. Options at this point are to create a new world, revisit and work on worlds that already have been created, or explore the worlds of others. To create a world, users click on one of several templates, which are full-color backgrounds or backdrops for the animated action. Once a scene is chosen, it appears in the upper-left corner of the next window, which is dominated by the code editor. This is the main workspace in Alice, where users build programs.

Once a world template, or background, has been chosen, Alice automatically includes a camera as an object in the world being created. Unlike other objects (characters, props) programmed to act and interact in animated movies that users create, the camera is not represented visually on-screen by an icon or avatar. Instead, it is an off-screen presence that records the action on-screen, just as a movie camera captures the work of actors while not being in the scene itself. The camera dictates point of view, meaning how and from what angles an audience sees the action that is taking place when watching the animated movie.

The camera can be controlled by arrows at the bottom of the window, which displays the world as it is being programmed. (More on this window, called the scene editor, later.) These arrow controls make the camera move left, right, forward, and backward—or rotate from a fixed location, as if the camera were on a stationary tripod. As with other objects in a world, the camera has a number of methods attached to it, which are instructions that change the camera angle, essentially allowing the camera to move from one fixed point to another.

>> LIGHTS, CAMERA, ALICE

Alice features a number of elements and terms that users might expect to encounter on a Hollywood soundstage. This is a nod to the way that users create animated movies while they learn programming.

In a movie, a continuous sequence of events is referred to as a scene. Likewise, virtual worlds in Alice contain scenes where objects move and interact in a continuous fashion. The scene editor is the workspace wherein users can view and test what they are creating. Scenes are populated with objects, which for movie-making purposes could be considered actors (characters) and props (furniture, buildings, etc.).

Movie actors follow a script, which is the written storyline with dialogue and direction. In Alice, the program is often referred to as the script; objects follow the script as written by the user/programmer.

The user/programmer plays many roles in this movie-making scenario. Taking the movie analogy even further, the user is like a screenwriter, casting agent, and director all rolled into one.

CALLING ALL METHODS

Also appearing in the opening window is the methods panel. To build programs, users drag method tiles—graphic blocks with the programming code written into them—from the methods panel onto the code editor.

As mentioned briefly, methods are statements that control how objects behave. In programming, instructing a computer to execute (meaning perform or carry out) a statement as programmed by the user is referred to as "calling a method." When Alice users call a method, it is as if they are sending a message

>> A computer programmer at work. A variety of elements used by programmers everywhere, including methods, are part of Alice software.

to an object in their worlds to make the object move or perform some other task.

In the methods panel are two tabs, one for procedures and the other for functions. Procedures are methods that perform an action, such as moving forward and turning. Functions are methods that ask questions about certain parts of an object and return a value

Each object in Alice has a predetermined set of methods built into it. Users are able to discover what methods are available to a specific object by clicking on that character or item in the object tree, which is a list of all the objects that have been placed in a scene. It is possible to create new methods for objects in Alice, but beginning users should find the number and variety of methods built in for each object to be more than enough to create interesting animated worlds.

Computer programmers everywhere use methods, procedures, and functions, whether they are working on Alice or another platform or computer language. Using these terms and including these elements as part of the Alice platform is one of the subtle ways that the software's creators teach users to think and act like programmers.

IN CONTROL OF THE SITUATION

A toolbar runs across the top left of the window in which the code editor appears, while the bottom-right portion is home to the control panel. This panel contains tiles that, appropriately enough, control methods, typically in one of two ways. Some of the tiles dictate the order in which methods occur, or how the action in an animation should take place. For instance, there are control tiles labeled "do in order" and "do together." Other tiles in this panel control how the program manages data, which is the information that makes the program run. Telling the program to set aside memory for storing data (the "variable" tile) and delegating which data should go into which storage space (the "assign" tile) are examples of management controls.

>> VARIABLES, PARAMETERS, AND LOOPING

Among the programming terms and concepts that Alice teaches in the course of building a world are variables, parameters, and looping.

Variables are spaces in which programmers store data—specifically a value, which is a specific quantity of data. One computer programmer suggests thinking of a variable as the memory function on a calculator, where users can store sums and figures for later use.

Like variables, parameters hold space in a program, but they are more like placeholders than memory keepers. For instance, if a programmer writes a method that can calculate the square root of any given number, he or she would leave a blank space in the program for various numbers for which the square root needs to be calculated. Then, when it comes time to use that method, the blank space needs to be filled in with whatever number for which the square root will be calculated. That blank space is a parameter.

Looping, which is also referred to as recursion, is the repeated use of information. When a programmer instructs the computer to keep running a particular method until another method is added to the program, it is called looping. This concept is useful for programmers using traditional coding because they do not have to write the same code over and over again.

MAKING A SCENE

Virtual worlds in Alice are made up of animations called scenes. The scene editor is where users can view and test the animations that are built by dragging and dropping method tiles onto the code editor. Because users work in both the code editor and the scene editor as they build programs, Alice has included buttons that allow them to easily toggle between the two. The editor in which users are working enlarges and becomes the main focus of the window, while the other editor remains on-screen but as a smaller auxiliary panel.

The scene editor is made up of two panels. One is the scene setup panel, which gives users the ability to change various object properties. Size and color are two of the properties that can be manipulated using the scene setup panel menu. An object's position can also be altered by keying numbers into a menu item or adding handles controlled by the computer's mouse; both methods are available on the scene

>> The click of a mouse allows users of Alice to drag and drop method tiles, as well as move items around within a scene.

setup panel. The second panel connected to the scene editor is the gallery.

CLASS ACT

A movie without characters and props is little more than a screen filled with static, or motionless, scenery. Animation requires movement and interaction by objects that populate users' virtual worlds. Anticipating such a need, Alice comes preloaded with a gallery of 3-D models—digital representations of characters and props—that are ready to be dragged and dropped into whatever worlds users create and programmed into action. The gallery that is accessed through the scene editor is called the local gallery, meaning it is part of the downloaded software. Models for use in Alice may also be found on the Internet in a Web gallery, but the software's creators suggest that the local gallery has more than enough models to make a beginning programmer happy.

>> Students can benefit from the assistance of a teacher when learning Alice, but users can experiment by themselves as well.

Finding just the right object for a scene is easy because of the way in which the Alice gallery is set up. Hundreds of objects are categorized into classes organized by mode of mobility, meaning the way in which they move: bipeds (two-legged creatures), quadrupeds (objects that move around on four legs), flyers, and swimmers. A fifth class is for props, such as buildings, trees, etc. Users may browse the different class folders to find object models for their animations, or they can perform a name-specific search by using the search box at the top right of each open gallery folder.

>> Importing MP3 files of a user's favorite tunes can bring a personalized finishing touch to animations created using Alice.

NOW HEAR THIS

Unlike blockbuster films playing at the local cineplex, movies made using Alice don't have access to Dolby stereo technology. They do, however, have sound capability. Sound effects and bits of dialogue can be imported using files from Alice's sound gallery.

Users may also import their own .wav or MP3 sound files, provided they use an outside audio editor, such as the Alice-recommended Audacity, to record the files. Using an outside editor helps ensure that no sound problems are encountered during playback of the animation.

FROM ALICE 1 THROUGH THE LOOKING GLASS

At the heart of Alice programming software is the ability of users to tell stories. Of course, Alice has a story of its own, chock full of information about how it came to be and the many ways the platform has changed through the years. From the very first version of 3-D software, designed as a virtual-reality program at the University of Virginia, through the offshoot teaching tool for middle schoolers called Looking Glass, Alice has a long and storied history of teaching beginners of all ages to program.

Together, the original Alice, Alice 2, and Alice 3 are known as the Alice Suite of educational tools. Storytelling Alice and Looking Glass are auxiliary programs, or offshoots of the Alice Suite software.

KEEPING IT REAL

The very first version of Alice was conceived at the University of Virginia in 1993. Its creator, Professor Randy Pausch, brought his design for Alice with him when he took a job teaching at

>> Carnegie Mellon p rofessor Randy Pausch was the mastermind behind Alice. Here, he delivers his now-famous "Achieving Your Childhood Dreams" lecture at the university on September 18, 2007.

Carnegie Mellon University in 1997. The software was designed for graduate students studying virtual reality (VR), or creating 3-D computer images that make users feel as if they are in a whole new world. This is the same technology that makes computer gamers feel as if they are right in the middle of the action, instead of simply sitting in front of a screen using a controller.

>> THE NEXT BIG VIRTUAL THING

VR technology helps users become immersed in a world of life-sized 3-D graphics, or objects. Specialized gear, such as a headset and a computerized data glove, allows users to move around in the simulated world and interact with objects therein in real time.

VR has been around since the late 1950s, when it was used mainly for flight and vehicle simulation exercises conducted by the U.S. military and NASA. Advanced computer capability and an interest in human-computer interaction (HCI) in the 1980s greatly increased the general public's knowledge of, and interest in, VR. By the time the Alice rapid prototyping system was created in the 1990s, computer scientists still had hopes that VR could become a form of electronic entertainment in and of itself, like computer gaming.

Alas, costs and other technological factors have put that dream on indefinite hold. Yet the work done on VR systems has not gone to waste. The 3-D technology that makes VR possible has been adapted and used by movie studios, computer game manufacturers, and computer programming environments such as Alice.

The original Alice, sometimes referred to as Alice 1, was what is known as a rapid prototyping system. The term refers to a system that combines programming language and tools so that a mock-up version of a program can be created in a short amount of time. The advantage of being able to watch the mock-up version of a program being played out on a screen is that users can spot problems and glitches in the programming right away.

In designing the Alice rapid prototyping system, its creators hoped to make virtual-reality programming easier for folks interested in the field but with little to no experience. As stated in the abstract to a 1995 article that appeared in *IEEE Computer Graphics and Applications*, Pausch and his team members at Carnegie Mellon University believed that "the best way to accelerate development in a new medium such as VR is to provide tools that allow people without highly technical backgrounds to create programs for it. These novice authors must be able to quickly try different nuances of an idea. They must be able to easily ask 'what if' questions."

Alice scripting was written in the Python programming language. As a "high-level" interpreted programming language, Python is easier for beginners to use because it uses simpler syntax in its code and runs commands quicker than a traditional language, such as C or C++.

At first Alice was used only within Carnegie Mellon University, as part of the Building Virtual Worlds course, originally taught by Pausch. The alpha, or very first, version of Alice 1 meant for public, desktop consumption was released in 1996, and the beta version, for testing with customers, followed in August 1997. The system, which was available as a free Internet download, ran on Windows 95. The original Alice is no longer available or in use; in the Building Virtual Worlds course, it has been supplanted by Panda software.

ALICE, TAKE TWO

Although virtual reality never really took off as a popular pastime in and of itself, the 3-D technology developed for the Alice rapid prototyping system did not go to waste. Carnegie Mellon computer science professors Pausch, Wanda Dann, and Stephen Cooper joined forces. Along with a team of other professors and graduate students, they created the Alice 2.0 programming environment.

In addition to the use of 3-D technology, Alice 2.0 had other things in common with the original Alice. First and foremost was the shared belief that beginning programmers would be best served by technology that was easy to use. Making Alice 2.0 an object-oriented environment that would give users quick, visual feedback on the programs they were creating was a must.

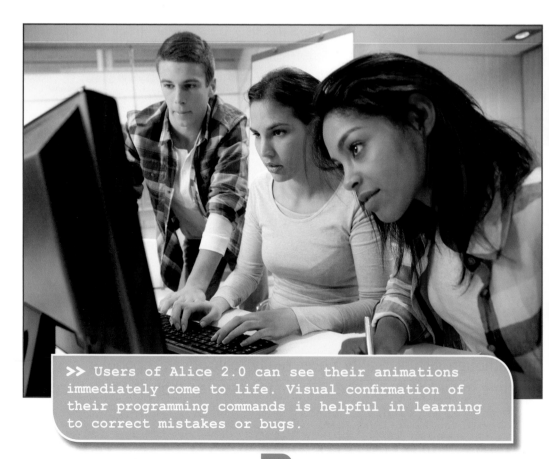

>> Users of Alice 2.0 can see their animations immediately come to life. Visual confirmation of their programming commands is helpful in learning to correct mistakes or bugs.

Rather than using Python as the programming language, the team behind Alice 2.0 used Java for the script. Python was, and still is, a great language for beginning programmers, but Java was chosen largely because it can run on more operating systems than Python. So the creators opted for making the environment available to more users overall instead of sticking with a language that had a much more forgiving learning curve. Besides, thanks to the use of prewritten code in graphic tiles, Alice 2.0 didn't need to worry as much about Java being slightly more difficult to learn than Python. Prewritten is still easier than keying in even simple coding.

Next, Alice 2.0 arrived on the scene as open-source, downloadable software. Like Alice 1, this version was designed for undergraduate college students who were taking introductory computer science courses. According to the team at Carnegie Mellon University, Alice 2.0 caught on in high school classrooms across the United States as well. Several other minor versions were released, each featuring changes that made the software perform better and worked out bugs in the system as they appeared.

No software is perfect. Carnegie Mellon University maintains pages on the Alice site listing known technical problems, or bugs. One Alice 2.0 bug involved users having trouble getting Alice to run after download. This was believed to have been caused by strengthened malware protection installed in most operating systems, which was interpreting the "nonstandard" Alice download as a threat. A workaround, which is an alternative way to get something done without making a major fix, was offered for this issue. Another bug had to do with accessing the Alice download from a networked computer.

THIRD TIME'S THE CHARM

Spurred on by the positive reception that Alice 2.0 and its sub-versions received, the Carnegie Mellon team began to investigate ways to make their programming software even better. Alice 3.0 was introduced in a beta, or test, version in 2009, and was officially released in 2012. While still geared toward college students,

>> ALICE, MEET THE SIMS

When comparing objects in the Alice gallery to characters created by animation giant Pixar, Randy Pausch had said of the former, "It's 3-D characters, but it's obviously low-budget." He was understandably thrilled, then, when computer game developer Electronic Arts (EA) agreed to feature art from its popular *The Sims* franchise in Alice software, starting with version 3.0.

The Sims art gave more definition to the facial features of Alice's human characters, which allowed objects to express emotions as a way to better tell a user's story. Movement also became much more fluid and natural looking. Incorporating the art into Alice meant rewriting code from C to Java, as well as protecting EA's rights to *The Sims* characters while keeping Alice open-source and available to everyone.

"Getting the chance to use the characters and animations from *The Sims* is like teaching at an art school and having Disney give you Mickey Mouse," said Pausch. "*The Sims* is EA's 'crown jewel,' and the fact that they are willing to use it for education shows a kind of long-term vision one rarely sees from large corporations."

3.0 was also intended to be used by high school students looking to gain experience in programming. Once 3.0 was introduced, the focus of Alice 2.0—which was not replaced by 3.0, as planned, but left available as part of the Alice Suite—moved to middle school and lower-level high school students.

Among the improvements and upgrades made to this version of Alice were sharper 3-D graphics in the objects gallery, particularly the addition of *Sims* characters to the human biped objects. Alice 3.0 also offered a way to view what the programming script would look like in Java and included a feature that let users share their worlds on YouTube.

>> Alice 3.x has made it easier for users who are particularly proud of their programming work to show off their animations on the popular sharing Web site YouTube.

Bugs attributed to Alice 3.1 have included getting the software to run after being downloaded from the Internet and running it on networked computers—bugs that were noted with Alice 2.3 as well. Other recorded trouble spots with Alice 3.1 have involved Java error messages. As was the case with Alice 2×, any bugs in the newest version were investigated and addressed as they arose.

ALICE SPINOFFS

Computer scientists have realized that to boost the number of computer science majors, it's important to get kids interested in programming at an early age. It was with this thought in mind that Caitlin Kelleher, a Carnegie Mellon University graduate student who had worked on Alice 2.0, developed an offshoot of Alice aimed specifically at middle school students, particularly young girls. Storytelling Alice shared much of the same code as Alice 2.0. It also used the same hook to capture the attention of users: the ability to animate stories in a 3-D environment.

Some teachers have noted that the objects in Storytelling Alice seemed to be richer than those in Alice 2.3, and they had more methods built into them that would allow users to tell a better story. Another interesting difference was that Storytelling Alice was not designed for use in a classroom with a teacher leading students in various projects. Instead, software users were offered online tutorials, which allowed them to experiment and work at their own pace. Finally, because Kelleher was working on the software as part of her graduate degree program and not for extended use by the general public, Storytelling Alice is available only on computers that run Windows.

>> Young girls were the target audience for Storytelling Alice, an offshoot of Alice 2.0 created by a former Carnegie Mellon graduate student.

After she had graduated and taken a position with Washington University in St. Louis, Missouri, Kelleher refined Storytelling Alice to create Looking Glass. Based on Storytelling Alice, Looking Glass gives users the ability to learn from programs previously created by their peers and, therefore, doesn't need to be taught in the classroom under the supervision of a teacher.

Storytelling Alice is no longer supported, meaning there is not a team making improvements to the software. The software is still available for downloading, though, on the Alice Web site, at www.alice.org/kelleher/storytelling. Because it is unsupported, Kelleher and the Alice team at Carnegie Mellon University strongly suggest that users download Looking Glass instead.

CHAPTER 4

BRANCHING OUT

Alice Educational Software was created as a way to get students interested in—and stay interested in—computer science and programming. Research seems to show that the software's creators were successful in their attempts. A study supported by the National Science Foundation showed that students who had poor math skills and/or no experience with programming performed well in computer science (CS) classes after taking a class using Alice. These at-risk students raised their grades from a C average to a B, and 88 percent of them went on to take more CS courses. The previous retention rate for at-risk students had been only 47 percent.

The numbers supporting the offshoot Storytelling Alice software are equally impressive. Creator Caitlin Kelleher reported that students who use Storytelling Alice log in 42 percent more time programming than users of Alice 2.0. Additionally, the Storytelling users were more likely to sneak in extra programming time than traditional Alice users.

Based on successes such as these, the creators and caretakers of Alice expanded the role of their 3-D programming environment as an educational tool. Competitions and special projects that incorporated use of the software began to emerge. Alice and those who created and refined it began to be recognized by educators, students, corporations, and the public at large, receiving a fair share of awards and grants along the way.

AN ONLINE SHOWCASE FOR PROGRAMMING SKILLS

Carrying forward its mission to strengthen the number of students pursuing degrees in computer science and other technology-related disciplines, Carnegie Mellon University has partnered with the Defense Advanced Research Projects Agency to create the Computer Science Student Network, known as CS2N. The research project is designed to help CS teachers supplement their lesson plans with online assignments and challenges that can be completed using the Alice Suite of programming tools.

The CS2N Web site features tutorials and games that cover material found in general computer science and programming curricula. Different programming and simulated environment tools are used to complete activities. In addition to modules centered on robotics, computer game design, and Web design, the CS2N site also supports activities on storytelling, animation, and programming, which prominently feature the use of Carnegie Mellon's own Alice 2x and 3x software. Students earn virtual badges for completing assignments, and themed competitions let them test their skills against those of others at their learning level.

>> ALICE GOES INTERNATIONAL

Riding the wave of animation popularity, educators in South America have started their own Alice-oriented events. Among these are themed competitions in Brazil and Argentina.

Begun in 2009, the Festival Animalice was inspired by Brazil's international animation festival, Anima Mundi. Using Alice software, teams of four to five participants script and program animations that not only address the theme chosen by organizers, but also meet several set technical requirements. In some competitions, participants also act as judges as they give feedback on the work of others.

Argentina's Sadosky Foundation is a public-private institution dedicated to strengthening ties between the worlds of school and work in the information and communications technology fields. The foundation sponsors a national competition, Challenge Dale Aceptar, which requires students to design animations and games using Alice software. More than twelve thousand secondary school students participated in the 2013 edition of the challenge.

FIRE UP THE ROBOTS

Computer science and robotics go hand in hand. Computer code and programming are what make robots work, after all. It makes sense, then, that the Carnegie Mellon School of Computer Science would be involved, along with the university's Robotics Academy, in a program called Fostering Innovation through Robotics Exploration (FIRE).

>> A robotics team celebrates at an ILITE (Inspiring Leaders in Technology and Engineering) event. Alice software is a notable presence at similar events hosted by Fostering Innovation through Robotics Exploration.

FIRE takes a layered approach to teaching technology, science, and mathematics. The concept is that by capitalizing on the more fun aspects of technology, such as robotics, educators will convince more people to study computer science and similar disciplines and pursue STEM (science, technology, engineering, and mathematics) careers. Alice's major contribution to ensuring the success of FIRE has been adding virtual worlds, much like the worlds created by Alice software, to the Robotics Academy's specialized programming language, ROBOTC. Additionally, the Alice team has sponsored an animation competition in conjunction with robotics competitions, which are the main thrust of the program.

I DREAM OF FINCH

It's one thing to make a robot object move around in a virtual world. It's something else to move a physical robot in the real world using a computer program. Alice is able to do both, the latter due to an invention called the Finch and the Finch Dreams programming environment.

The Finch, a small robot that looks a bit like a stingray but with a thicker tail, is a project of the CREATE (Community Robotics, Education, and Technology Empowerment) lab at Carnegie Mellon University. In order to make programming even more fun, the Alice team designed a version of its software that lets users write interactive programs that activate a series of sensors on the Finch robot, as well as make it roll around on its wheels.

Users place a virtual Finch in a newly created Alice world and run the Finch Dreams program with drag-and-drop tiles, just as they would with other Alice software. Instead of making the on-screen, virtual robot move, however, the methods in the program make the physical Finch move and respond with sounds and lights.

The Finch, which runs by way of a cable plugged into its USB port, can also play sound files, receive RSS feeds from the Internet, and use an attached Web cam. Dozens of suggested programming assignments come with the robot. Unlike the open-source Alice software that runs it, the Finch is not free—the suggested retail price is $99.

THE FBI'S MOST WANTED... SOFTWARE

In 2010, the Alice team partnered with the Federal Bureau of Investigation (FBI) to help get the word out about dangers lurking on the Internet. Student programmers using Alice entered a national competition to create short animations for the bureau's Safe Online Surfing (SOS) program. The project has become an annual event and is referred to as the FBI's "Alice Challenge."

Middle school and high school students participate in the competition, aimed at delivering an online safety message to children in grades three through eight. Organizers believe that the use of animation will appeal to the target audience, as will the fact that the forty-five-second films were created by programmers who are essentially their peers. The FBI presents awards to winning animations at the middle school and high school levels.

In a press release, Wanda Dann, head of the Alice Project, said, "In this collaboration, teachers and students will work together to learn safe surfing techniques. By using our Alice software to create 3-D animations, students can then use their imaginations and creativity to spread this message even further and perhaps even more effectively."

ALICE GOES TO SUMMER CAMP

Since 2006, Duke University has brought Alice into dozens of U.S. classrooms through its Adventures in Alice project. Teachers from middle schools and high schools primarily in North Carolina, where Duke is located, receive training, guidance, and materials to help them become well versed in the Alice programming environment.

Teachers attend summer workshops that introduce them to the Alice Suite and help them hone their own programming skills. After the workshops are completed, the educators devise lesson plans for teaching Alice to students. They are able to test their skills by helping middle school and high school students who attend a weeklong Alice camp that is held at the same location as the teacher workshops.

Once they return to their classrooms, teachers receive online support from Duke's Adventures in Alice Web site, at http://www.cs.duke.edu/csed/alice/aliceInSchools. Lesson plans submitted at various workshops, free tutorials, and information about upcoming Alice workshops and conferences are posted on the site.

Adventures in Alice was originally supposed to run for only three years, through 2009. Realizing the value of the project, however, Duke applied for and received a $2.5 million National Science Foundation grant to continue the program through 2016.

ACCOLADES ABOUND

Those involved with the Alice programming environment, from its creation to the present day, have made the project a labor of love. Their main goal was to make programming easier and more fun for beginners, not to win praise for their work. Yet they have been the recipients of several grants and awards over the years, as has the programming system itself.

Among the awards given to Randy Pausch, who is considered the father of the Alice Suite, was the 2007 Karl V. Karlstrom Outstanding Educator Award, presented by the Association for Computing Machinery (ACM). He was selected

>> The goal of making computer programming easy for novice users has been met by the team behind the development of Alice Educational Software.

for his contributions toward making computer science fun and accessible to students of all skill levels. The awards committee noted Pausch's creation of Alice, as well as his Building Virtual Worlds course and the cofounding of Carnegie Mellon University's Entertainment Technology Center.

His Alice-chief successor, Wanda Dann, was also recognized for excellence in teaching with the presentation of ACM's 2012 Distinguished Educator Award. The award recognizes "singular impacts on the dynamic computing field." Also receiving a Distinguished Educator Award that year from ACM was Stephen Cooper, a Stanford University professor whose work on Alice and Alice-related materials extends back to the early days of the software's development, when he was employed by St. Joseph's University in Philadelphia, Pennsylvania.

Although she worked on Alice 2.0 as a graduate student, it was for her later work on developing Looking Glass that Caitlin Kelleher received a 2011 National Science Foundation CAREER Award. Given to teachers early in their careers, the award recognizes those who have combined outstanding research with inspired teaching. Kelleher also received a two-year, $50,000 fellowship from the Alfred P. Sloan Foundation to advance her work on Looking Glass and other projects.

Finally, in 2009, Alice won the Duke's Choice Award for Java Technology in Education. Presented by Sun Microsystems, the award recognizes the most influential computer applications using Java, the programming language on which Alice is based. Apparently, Sun Microsystems was suitably impressed with Alice even before giving it the Duke's Choice Award. The year before, the company had pledged financial support toward Carnegie Mellon University's efforts to globalize Alice, meaning it would provide tools to help translate the platform into other languages and otherwise make the system understandable to people from various cultures.

>> Awards and praise of the past have allowed the creators of Alice to look to the future with great confidence and the thrill of remarkable expectations.

THE FUTURE LOOKS BRIGHT

As announced in an April 2013 press release, Oracle Academy and the educational resources nonprofit Curriki have designed a curriculum around Alice that they hope to make available to high school students worldwide. The curriculum would help teachers guide students through the learning process. Oracle, a company dedicated to simplifying information technology, has been a supporter of the Alice Project at Carnegie Mellon University for years.

The attention and praise given to Alice, past and present, indicates that the software has lived up to its promise to make programming fun and easy. Like the character Alice in Lewis Carroll's book, Alice the programming environment has success-fully navigated new worlds, experiencing quite an adventure along the way.

AUXILIARY Offering help in a secondary capacity.

BUG A trouble spot or error in a computer program, usually related to faulty code.

FUNCTION In programming, instructions regarding the performance of a task that asks and answers a question before the task can be performed.

INTEGRATED DEVELOPMENT ENVIRONMENT (IDE) An environment, or system, that lets users write programs and run them in one package.

LOGIC In computer programming, the way in which commands are arranged that determines how a computer performs tasks.

LOOPING The repeated use of information in a computer program.

METHOD A programming statement that tells objects on a computer screen how to act.

NOVICE Someone who is a beginner at a task or activity.

OBJECT In programming, a collection of data stored in a computer's memory, represented as a character or other on-screen figure.

OPEN SOURCE A program offered to anyone and everyone without a license or fee.

PARAMETER A placeholder in a computer program's code where users fill in data to execute a command.

PLATFORM A standard way of operating around which software can be developed.

PROGRAMMING The process of creating and running a set of instructions that make a computer perform certain tasks and functions.

PROPERTIES The information in a program that defines an object.

RAPID PROTOTYPING A system that lets users create a quick mock-up, or model, version of a program.

SUPPLEMENT Something that is added to strengthen or extend the original.

SYNTAX In programming, the rules that determine the order in which code must be placed for a program to run smoothly, or at all.

TEMPLATE A document or compilation of data that is formatted a specific way and can be used repeatedly.

TOGGLE To switch back and forth between screens or other features on a computer using certain keystrokes or commands.

TRIPOD A support for a camera that stands on three legs.

VARIABLE A space in a computer program that is saved in the computer's memory for future use.

VIRTUAL REALITY A system using three-dimensional computer images and sound to create an artificial environment that feels real to the user.

Canadian Computer Society
260 Adelaide Street East, No. 210
Toronto, ON M5A 1N1
Canada
(416) 299-5282
E-mail: membership@cancomputes.com
Web site: http://www.cancomputes.com
The Canadian Computer Society offers information, conducts
    research, and promotes study in all areas of computer
    technology.

Carnegie Mellon University
School of Computer Science
5000 Forbes Avenue
Pittsburgh, PA 15213
(412) 268-2565
Web site: http://www.cs.cmu.edu
Seeking to attract and retain more students studying in STEM
    fields, the School of Computer Science offers undergradu-
    ate and graduate courses in disciplines such as computing,
    information technology, and robotics. Past and current
    faculty members have played a vital role in the creation and
    maintenance of Alice.

Computing in the Core
1101 Vermont Avenue NW, Suite 400
Washington, DC 20005
(202) 349-2333

Web site: http://www.computinginthecore.org

Computing in the Core is a coalition of associations, corporations, scientific societies, and other nonprofits working to make computer science education part of the K–12 core curriculum in the United States.

Educational Computing Organization of Ontario

10 Morrow Avenue, Suite 202

Toronto, ON M6R 2J1

Canada

(416) 538-1650

Web site: http://www.ecoo.org

Established in 1979, the Educational Computing Organization of Ontario is a nonprofit that facilitates the integration of new computing technology, such as Alice, into the educational curriculum.

National Association of Programmers (NAP)

P.O. Box 529

Prairieville, LA 70769

Web site: http://napusa.org

Formed in 1995, the National Association of Programmers is a professional organization dedicated to programmers, developers, consultants, and other professionals and students in the computer industry. It offers certification programs, conferences, and publications to its members.

Washington University in St. Louis

Computer Science and Engineering

1 Brookings Drive
St. Louis, MO 63130
Web site: http://cse.wustl.edu
The Computer Science and Engineering department at Washington University promotes novel uses of information technology across a wide range of disciplines. Caitlin Kelleher, who worked on Alice 2.0, created Looking Glass while working as a professor at the university.

WEB SITES

Due to the changing nature of Internet links, Rosen Publishing has developed an online list of Web sites related to the subject of this book. This site is updated regularly. Please use this link to access the list:

http://www.rosenlinks.com/CODE/Alice

Burd, Barry. *Beginning Programming with Java for Dummies.* Hoboken, NJ: Wiley, 2012.

Dann, Wanda P., Stephen Cooper, and Randy Pausch. *Learning to Program with Alice.* Upper Saddle River, NJ: Prentice Hall, 2011.

Freedman, Jerri. *Careers in Computer Science and Programming.* New York, NY: Rosen Publishing, 2011.

Furgang, Kathy. *Careers in Digital Animation.* New York, NY: Rosen Publishing, 2012.

Gaddis, Tony. *Starting Out with Alice.* 3rd ed. Boston, MA: Addison-Wesley, 2012.

Hardnett, Charles R. *Programming Like a Pro for Teens.* Boston, MA: Cengage Learning, 2012.

Marinelli, Donald. *The Comet & the Tornado: Reflections on the Legacy of Randy Pausch.* New York, NY: Sterling Publishing, 2010.

Pausch, Randy, and Jeffrey Zaslow. *The Last Lecture.* New York, NY: Hyperion, 2008.

Peddie, Jon. *The History of Visual Magic in Computers: How Beautiful Images Are Made in CAD, 3D, VR and AR.* New York, NY: Springer Publishing, 2013.

Rogler, Harold L. *Alice Programming.* Dubuque, IA: Kendall Hunt Publishing, 2013.

Sande, Warren, and Sande Carter. *Hello World! Computer Programming for Kids and Other Beginners.* Shelter Island, NY: Manning Publications, 2013.

Strom, Chris. *3D Programming for Kids: Create Interactive Worlds with JavaScript.* Raleigh, NC: The Pragmatic Bookshelf, 2013.

Carnegie Mellon University. "Alice." Retrieved October 2013
(http://www.alice.org).

Dann, Wanda, et. al. "Alice 3 How-To Guide." Alice.org, May
2012. Retrieved October 2013 (http://www.alice.org/3.1/
Materials/HowToGuide/HowToGuide_PDF_Complete.pdf).

Herbert, Charles W. *An Introduction to Alice and Object-
Oriented Programming*. Independence, KY: Cengage
Learning, 2007.

Lewis, John, and Peter DePasquale. *Programming With
Alice and Java*. Boston, MA; Addison Wesley Publishing
Co., 2008.

Mims, Christopher. "Whatever Happened to ... Virtual Reality?"
MIT Technology Review, October 2010. Retrieved October
2013 (http://www.technologyreview.com/view/421293/
whatever-happened-to-virtual-reality/).

Pausch, Randy, et. al. "A Brief Architectural Overview of Alice,
a Rapid Prototyping System for Virtual Reality." *IEEE
Computer Graphics and Applications*, Vol. 15, Issue 3,
pp. 8-11; May 1995.

Science Daily. "Alice Teaches Kids to Program: Computer
Scientists Develop New Kid-Friendly Programming
Language." October 2007. Retrieved September 2013
(http://www.sciencedaily.com/videos/2007/1012-alice
_teaches_kids_to_program.htm).

Science Daily. "Bringing Boys and Girls To Computer Science with
'Alice.'" July 2009. Retrieved October 2013 (http://www
.sciencedaily.com/releases/2009/06/090623112115.htm).

{ INDEX

ABOUT THE AUTHOR

Jeanne Nagle is an author and editor based in upstate New York. Among the titles she has either written or edited are *Computing: From the Abacus to the iPad, Top STEM Careers in Technology, Issues in Cyberspace,* and *Careers in Internet Advertising and Marketing.*

PHOTO CREDITS

Cover © iStockphoto.com/JodiJacobson; p. 5 The Bridgeman Art Library/Getty Images; p. 8 Chris Schmidt/E+/Getty Images; p. 10 age fotostock/SuperStock; pp. 12, 26–27, 28–29 iStock/Thinkstock; p. 15 webphotographeer/E+/Getty Images; p. 20 © aberCPC/Alamy; p. 23 Janice Richard/E+/Getty Images; p. 30 Digital Vision/Photodisc/Thinkstock; p. 33 Pittsburgh Post-Gazette/ZUMA Press/Newscom; p. 36 Goodluz/Shutterstock.com; p. 39 © iStockphoto.com/Viktor Lugovskoy; p. 41 michaeljung/Shutterstock.com; pp. 46–47 Robotics Chelle Hambric, ILITE Robotics; p. 51 kali9/E+/Getty Images; p. 53 Nika Fadul/Flickr Select/Getty Images; cover and interior design elements © iStockphoto.com/letoakin (programming language), © iStockphoto.com/AF-studio (binary pattern), © iStockphoto.com/piccerella (crosshatch pattern).

Designer: Nicole Russo; Editor: Heather Moore Niver;
Photo Researcher: Karen Huang